YOUNG LEARNER'S ENCYCLOPEDIA

Written by:

Molly Perham
& Julian Rowe

Illustrated by:

Chris Leishman

Contents

© 2006 Alligator Books Limited
Published by Alligator Books Limited
Gadd House, Arcadia Avenue, London N3 2JU
Printed in China.

www.alligatorbooks.co.uk

OUR WORLD

Encyclopedias tell you all about our world. In this book you will find a different topic as you turn each page. At the back, the index shows exactly where you can find information.

A CENTURY OF DISCOVERY

In the 20th century, more changes have taken place in our world than at any other time in history. Explorers have reached the icy North and South poles, explored the depths of the oceans and travelled into space. Scientists have found wonderful uses for electricity and invented the microchip. Archaeologists have discovered how people lived in the past. Who knows what the 21st century will bring?

A WORLD OF INFORMATION

Before printing was invented, most people knew very little about the world outside their own village. Printed books made knowledge available to all. Now radio, television and computers bring us information at the press of a button. Jet aircraft carry us to the other side of the world in less than a day.

Modern communications have made our world a smaller place.

STRANGE BUT TRUE

Use the index at the back of the book to help you find the information you need.

★ Every minute of the day 404,690 sq. metres of tropical rainforest is destroyed. At this rate there will be no rainforest left in 40 years.

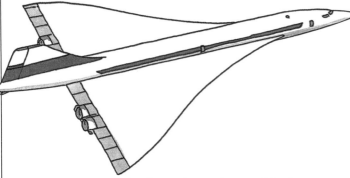

★ The Concorde flew from New York to London in just under three hours. Because of the time difference, you arrived in London an hour before you left New York.

TOMORROW'S WORLD

We depend on the land to produce enough food for everyone. We want to breathe clean air and drink pure water. Fossil fuels, such as oil and gasoline, will not last forever. As we learn more about our world, we understand how important it is to take care of it.

WORLD RECORDS

Antarctica contains 99 per cent of the world's ice.

The Pacific Ocean is almost as big as all the other oceans put together.

Pacific Ocean

The highest mountain is Mount Everest in Nepal. It is 8,848 metres high. The peak is often hidden in clouds.

In comparison to some of the other planets in the Solar System, our world is quite small. If you walked fast without stopping, you could walk right around the Equator in 250 days. It would take 10 times longer to walk around Saturn.

Equator

THE EARTH

Earth is one of nine planets circling the Sun. None of the others can support life.

Only the Earth has an atmosphere in which we can breathe, water to drink and plants and animals.

INSIDE THE EARTH

If you could cut the Earth in half, you would see that it is made up of layers. At the centre is a heavy, hot core of molten metal. Then there is a mantle of rock. The mantle is cooler than the core, and like thick syrup. The outer crust is the layer on which we live. Proportionately it is as thin as a coat of paint on a basketball.

Crust

Mantle

Core

EARTHQUAKES AND VOLCANOES

The thin crust of Earth's surface floats on the mantle. The crust moves constantly. Over time parts of it, called plates, slide or grate against each other and cause earthquakes. When a volcano erupts, hot molten rock and gases force their way up from below the crust. The red hot rock spews into the air. Molten rock flowing down from a volcano is called lava.

MOUNTAINS AND RIVERS

Sometimes the plates of Earth's crust collide. Over time, great mountain ranges are created. As rain falls it runs down mountains and hillsides forming streams and rivers. Some carve great canyons in the land. Rivers flow into lakes, oceans and seas.

ROCKS, MINING AND OIL

Rocks in the Earth's crust are used to make buildings and roads. Some rocks contain metal ores. These are mined to make metals such as iron and aluminium. Other rocks trap underground lakes of oil and natural gas.

VERY HOT AND VERY COLD

Deserts are dry because very little rain falls. During the day when it is very hot, the animals that live there have to find places to shelter from the Sun. Camels, which live in some deserts, can travel great distances without drinking water. Deserts can be cold at night.

Drilling deep into the Earth's crust brings the oil and gas to the surface.

STRANGE BUT TRUE

★ In Asia, people used to believe that the world was supported by a tortoise that lived on the backs of four elephants.

★ In 1968, three US astronauts became the first people to see the shape of the Earth with their own eyes. Before then, people had only seen parts of the Earth.

★ At the Equator, the Earth rotates at 1,609 km/h. Without the force of gravity, you would fly out into space.

At the North and South poles there is always snow and ice. Polar bears have thick fur coats to keep them warm.

THE SEA

F rom space, the world looks blue. This is because nearly three-quarters of its surface is covered with water. The four great oceans of the world are the Atlantic Ocean, the Pacific Ocean, the Indian Ocean and the Arctic Ocean.

HARVESTING THE SEAS

Great numbers of fish feed and breed in the shallow water that surrounds the continents. This is where fishing fleets do most of their fishing.

LOW TIDE, HIGH TIDE

Tides come in and go out twice a day at the seaside. They are caused by the Sun and the Moon attracting the sea towards them.

The sea comes much farther up the beach at high tide. The highest tides are in spring and autumn.

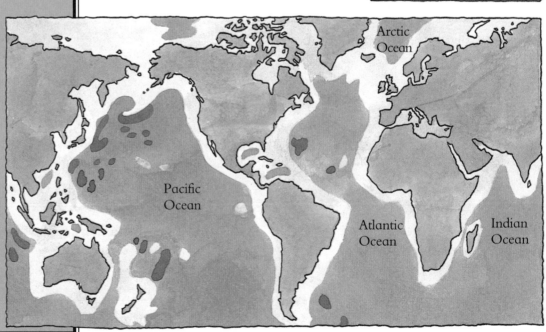

Arctic Ocean

Pacific Ocean

Atlantic Ocean

Indian Ocean

GIANTS OF THE OCEAN

Whales are the largest mammals. The blue whale, which is shown below, weighs more than 10,160 kilograms and is some 30 metres long. Killer whales hunt in groups and attack other whales as well as dolphins, seals and penguins. Squid, which can weigh 453 kilograms and measure more than 15 metres long, are the largest animals without a backbone.

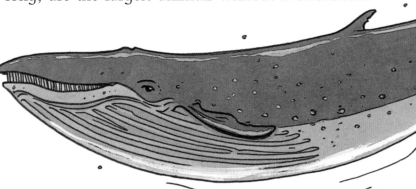

CORAL ISLANDS

Coral is the chalky skeleton of a tiny animal called a coral polyp. Each new polyp grows from the side of its parent. More and more coral builds up in the shallow warm sea water near islands. A large coral reef takes hundreds of years to grow. It provides a home for many sea creatures.

There is so much salt in the Dead Sea that you can sit up as you float.

STRANGE BUT TRUE

★ The Australian Great Barrier Reef is made of coral. It is 2,027 kilometres long, and can be seen from the Moon.

★ Eskimos use sea ice as a source of fresh water for drinking. When the surface of the sea freezes, the salt is left behind in the water.

Weather is part of our daily lives. It affects the way we dress, what we eat and how we spend our time.

In some parts of the world the weather stays much the same day after day. In others it is always changing.

THE ATMOSPHERE

Weather is caused by changes in the atmosphere – the blanket of air above the Earth. Clouds, rain, wind and heat waves are all produced in the bottom layer of the atmosphere, called the troposphere. Jet aircraft often fly above the clouds where the air is less active.

THE WIND

Weather changes are blown around the world by winds. Winds are formed when the Sun heats up some parts of the Earth more strongly than others, and the difference in heat makes the air move. Hurricanes and tornadoes form in warm, damp air when winds hurl into each other from opposite directions.

THE WATER CYCLE

The Sun heats the sea and turns some of it into water vapour, which rises into the sky to make a cloud. The wind blows the cloud across the sky. When the cloud reaches warm land it rises and meets cold air. This cools the cloud and turns the vapour into water again. The drops fall as rain, which trickles down the mountains and forms rivers. Water also filters through to the water table.

Water vapour

Water table

SNOW

If the air in a cloud is below freezing, some of the water vapour freezes into ice crystals. These crystals stick together to make snowflakes. Every snowflake has six points, but each one has a different shape.

STRANGE BUT TRUE

* You can work out how far away a storm is by counting the seconds between a flash of lightning and the roll of thunder. Five seconds equals 1.6 km.

* In the USA, hurricanes are given people's names in alphabetical order.

CLIMATE

Climate is the usual weather of an area over a long period of time. The weather may change from day to day, but the climate stays the same. An area's climate depends on how close it is to the Equator. Countries near the Equator get more of the Sun's rays and usually have a hotter climate than places farther north or south.

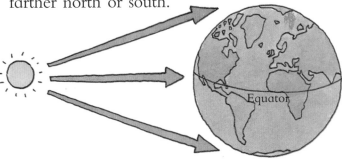

FORECASTING

Weather forecasters collect information and take measurements to provide a picture of how the atmosphere is behaving.

Red sky at night, sailor's delight. Red sky in the morning, sailor's warning.

STORMY WEATHER

Thunderstorms are caused by electricity in the air. The electrical charges that build up inside rain clouds make flashes of lightning. The worst type of storm is a hurricane, which can cause a lot of damage. Information sent back to Earth from satellites can help warn of a developing storm.

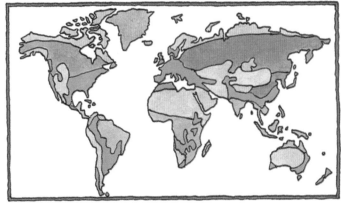

☐ **Polar**
Cold and dry. Always icy at the poles.

☐ **Cold forests**
Long snowy winters and short warm summers.

☐ **Temperate**
Not too hot nor too cold. Rain all year.

☐ **Dry**
Deserts very hot and dry all year, with hardly any rain. Mountain areas dry and cold.

☐ **Tropical**
Hot all year. Wet and dry seasons on the grasslands. Rainy all year in the forests. Hurricanes start in the tropics.

PLANTS

Garden flowers, vegetables, fruits and grasses are all flowering plants. Many trees and shrubs also have flowers.

Without plants there would be no food for animals to eat. Most plants produce flowers and seeds so they can reproduce. Plants are divided up into groups by the things they have in common. These groups are called families.

PARTS OF A FLOWERING PLANT

The flower attracts insects with its colour and scent. Insects carry pollen from the male part of the flower, called the stamen, to the female part, the pistil.

When a flower has been pollinated, it produces seeds from which new plants sprout and grow.

The leaves use sunlight to make food from air and water. This is called photosynthesis.

The stem carries food and water around the plant.

The roots hold the plant firmly in the ground. They suck in water and minerals from the soil.

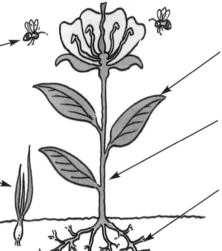

TRAPPING THE SUN'S ENERGY

Every living thing needs energy to keep it alive. Green plants trap the Sun's energy and make it into food. The energy in plant food passes on to the animals that eat the plants.

THE AIR WE BREATHE

Plants also provide the oxygen that we need to breathe. While making their food, plants take in the carbon dioxide gas that people and animals breathe out, and give off oxygen instead.

EVERGREEN TREES

Trees that do not lose their leaves in the fall are called evergreens. Evergreens actually lose their leaves throughout the year, but are continually growing new ones.

DECIDUOUS TREES

Many of the trees found in cool countries lose their leaves in the autumn. The leaves change colour, then drop off and rot on the ground. Trees that lose their leaves in this way are called deciduous.

TROPICAL RAINFORESTS

Tropical rainforests are very hot and there is heavy rain most days. Trees quickly grow very tall. Rainforests are home to many different animals and birds, and produce 50 per cent of the world's oxygen supply. In some parts of the world they are being destroyed. Many valuable plants are disappearing.

PLANTS WITHOUT FLOWERS

Algae are simple plants without flowers. The best known algae are seaweeds.

A fungus cannot make food for itself. It takes food from other living things, or from dead wood and leaves. Toadstools and mushrooms are fungi. Their caps produce spores that grow into new plants.

Mosses grow in damp places. They produce capsules on thin stalks. The capsules release powdery spores that grow into new plants.

Ferns have leaves, or fronds, which grow up from an underground stem. Spores are carried under the fronds.

STRANGE BUT TRUE

★ Many animals eat plants, but not many plants eat animals! An exception is the Venus flytrap, which catches insects between its leaves and uses them for food.

ANIMALS

An animal is any living thing that is not a plant. Nobody knows how many different animals there are. New kinds are discovered every year. Animals are divided into groups by their characteristics. Mammals were the last group to appear on Earth.

FISH

Fish are cold-blooded animals that live in the water. Fish have backbones and are called vertebrates. They swim by moving their tails from side to side. Fish breathe through gills on each side of the head. Most fish lay eggs, but some give birth to live young.

The ancestors of modern fish appeared on Earth over 500 million years ago.

AMPHIBIANS

Amphibians can live either in the water or on land. Like fish, amphibians are cold-blooded animals with backbones. They lay eggs in a layer of jelly which protects them.

Eggs

Life cycle of a frog

Growing tadpoles

REPTILES

A reptile is a cold-blooded animal that moves on its belly or its very short legs. For millions of years reptiles were the most numerous animals in the world. Now the only kinds left are tortoises and turtles, crocodiles and alligators, lizards and snakes. Reptiles, like all cold-blooded animals, get their warmth from the heat of the Sun.

BIRDS

Birds are warm-blooded animals. Some people believe they are descended from dinosaurs. Birds have feathers and wings. They have hollow bones so that they are light in the air, and strong breast muscles for flapping their wings. But some birds, like ostriches, cannot fly. Birds build nests, in which they lay eggs and raise their young.

INSECTS

Insects are invertebrates (animals without backbones). Instead of skeletons, their bodies are held together by a hard outer shell. All insects have three pairs of legs. Their bodies are divided into three parts: head, thorax and abdomen. Some insects (such as bees, which pollinate plants) are helpful to humans; others, like the mosquito, are considered pests.

STRANGE BUT TRUE

★ The tuatara has survived for 150 million years. This strange reptile lives on islands off the coast of New Zealand.

★ The echidna and the platypus are mammals, but they lay eggs.

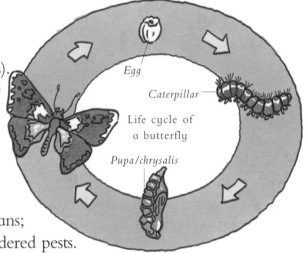

Egg

Caterpillar

Life cycle of a butterfly

Pupa/chrysalis

MAMMALS

Mammals have warm blood and a bony skeleton. Many have hair or fur on their bodies to keep them warm. Most mammals give birth to live babies, which are fed with milk produced by the mother. Marsupials, such as kangaroos, are carried in their mother's pouch until they are fully developed. The most intelligent mammals are the primates. This family includes monkeys, apes and humans.

A FOOD PYRAMID

In the African savanna, antelopes, wildebeest and zebra feed on grass and leafy shrubs. These herbivores are prey for the meat-eaters, or carnivores, such as lions.

PREHISTORIC TIMES

Most of the plants and animals that lived millions of years ago were quite different from those we know today. Scientists have discovered what they looked like by studying fossils preserved in rocks, and remains found in ice.

THE FIRST PLANTS

About 350 million years ago, great forests covered the Earth. Most of the plants were giant sized. When the plants died they fell into the swampy ground. Over millions of years they became buried under more dead trees and the plants turned into coal.

THE FIRST ANIMALS

The first living things existed over 1.5 billion years ago. They were simple creatures that lived in the sea. Fish appeared 1 billion years later. They were followed by amphibians and then reptiles.

TRILOBITES AND AMMONITES

Trilobites looked like large woodlice. The legs were used for walking on the bottom of the sea or for swimming. Ammonites had coiled shells. Some were very small and others grew as large as 2 metres long.

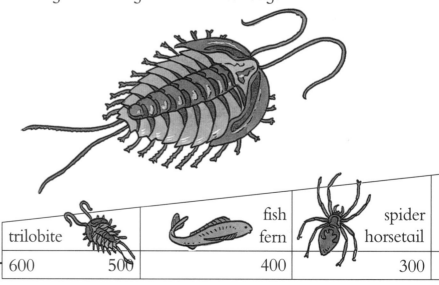

trilobite		fish fern	spider horsetail
600	500	400	300

Dinosaur means 'terrible lizard'.

STRANGE BUT TRUE

★ *Pachycephalosaurs* had very thick skulls. They were just like crash helmets. The males banged their heads together in fights.

FLYING REPTILES

The pterosaurs were flying reptiles. Their large wings stretched from a very long finger to the sides of the body and hind legs. The largest pterosaur was *Pteranodon*, which had a wingspan of 7.5 metres. The smallest was the size of a sparrow.

ARMOUR-PLATING

Stegosaurus and *Triceratops* were protected by armour. *Triceratops* had three horns and a bony frill across its neck. *Stegosaurus* had bony plates along its back.

DINOSAURS

Dinosaurs dominated the Earth for 140 million years. The largest were the four-footed vegetarian dinosaurs with long necks and tails. Other dinosaurs walked upright on their hind legs, with their very small front legs held off the ground. The largest of the two-legged dinosaurs was the fierce meat-eater, *Tyrannosaurus rex*.

WHY DID THEY DIE?

Dinosaurs and pterosaurs died out about 65 million years ago. What killed them remains one of the great puzzles of the past. Some scientists believe that the climate grew too cold for them to survive. Others believe an enormous asteroid hit the Earth and destroyed the dinosaurs. Their place was taken by a different group of animals, the warm-blooded mammals.

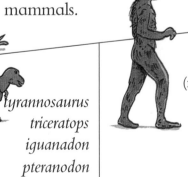

			Australopithecus (not quite a caveman)
	diplodocus	*tyrannosaurus*	ape
	stegosaurus	*triceratops*	butterfly
ammonite	*ichthyosaurus*	*iguanadon*	early horse
cycad	*archaeopteryx*	*pteranodon*	mammoth
dimetrodon			
200	135	65	1.8 million years ago

ANCIENT TIMES

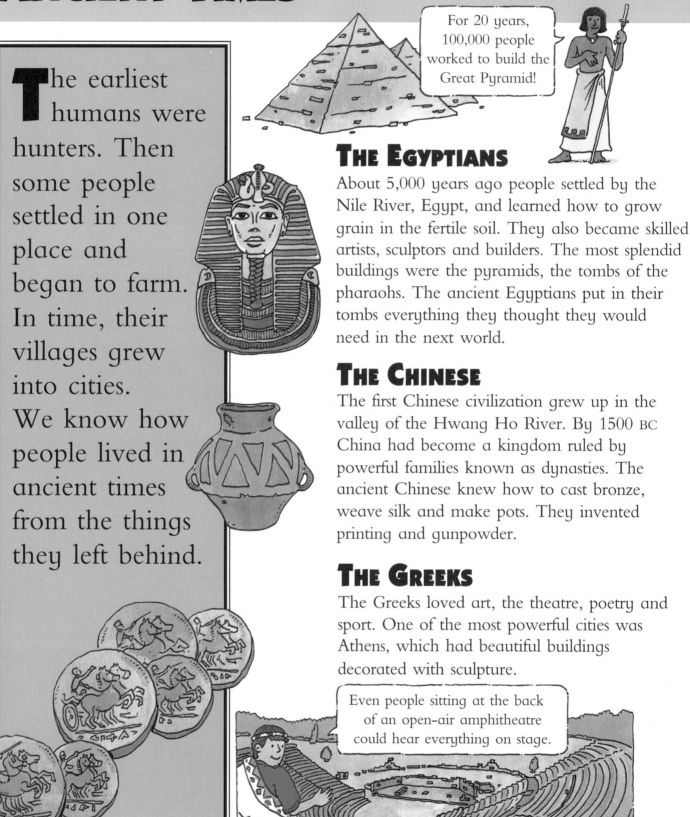

The earliest humans were hunters. Then some people settled in one place and began to farm. In time, their villages grew into cities. We know how people lived in ancient times from the things they left behind.

For 20 years, 100,000 people worked to build the Great Pyramid!

THE EGYPTIANS

About 5,000 years ago people settled by the Nile River, Egypt, and learned how to grow grain in the fertile soil. They also became skilled artists, sculptors and builders. The most splendid buildings were the pyramids, the tombs of the pharaohs. The ancient Egyptians put in their tombs everything they thought they would need in the next world.

THE CHINESE

The first Chinese civilization grew up in the valley of the Hwang Ho River. By 1500 BC China had become a kingdom ruled by powerful families known as dynasties. The ancient Chinese knew how to cast bronze, weave silk and make pots. They invented printing and gunpowder.

THE GREEKS

The Greeks loved art, the theatre, poetry and sport. One of the most powerful cities was Athens, which had beautiful buildings decorated with sculpture.

Even people sitting at the back of an open-air amphitheatre could hear everything on stage.

THE ROMANS

The Romans had a strong army and built up a vast empire around the Mediterranean Sea. Rome, in Italy, was the capital. For a time Rome was ruled by a government of senators until, in 49 BC, Julius Caesar made himself Emperor. The Romans were expert builders and engineers. Remains of their roads, villas, bridges and baths can still be found in Europe today.

THE INCAS

The Incas ruled a great empire in South America from AD 1200-1500. Cities like

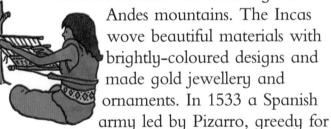

Machu Picchu were built high in the Andes mountains. The Incas wove beautiful materials with brightly-coloured designs and made gold jewellery and ornaments. In 1533 a Spanish army led by Pizarro, greedy for gold, conquered the Inca empire.

THE AZTECS

In 1345 a small tribe of hunters founded the city of Tenochtitlan on Lake Texcoco in Mexico. In less than 200 years they ruled an empire that stretched from coast to coast. The Aztecs were interested in astronomy and mathematics, and

developed their own calendar. Great temples were built to honour their many gods.

HOW THEY WROTE

Ancient Egyptian writing is called hieroglyphics.

The characters used in Chinese writing developed from early picture-writing.

Our alphabet comes from the Roman letters of 2,500 years ago.

Aa Bb Cc Dd Ee

STRANGE BUT TRUE

★ The Great Pyramid at Giza, Egypt, is 135 metres high and made of 2,300,000 blocks of stone. The ancient Egyptians had no cranes, so they may have dragged the blocks across rollers to pull the huge stones up a long ramp.

★ The Incas had no money and didn't write, but they kept accurate accounts by making knots in pieces of string, called quipus. These were also used to send messages.

			BC	AD	
5000	2000	1000	0		1000
Egyptians		Chinese	Greeks	Romans	Incas Aztecs

EXPLORERS

S ince ancient times, people have travelled and settled in different places. Many early explorers set out to find new lands and new people to trade with. Today nearly all of the world has been discovered and mapped by explorers who made dangerous voyages by sea, or journeys by land or air.

VIKINGS

The Vikings were sea warriors who sailed far in their magnificent longboats. From the 8th to the 11th century these Norsemen, or men from the North, terrorised Europe, taking slaves and stealing treasure from monasteries and churches. They were also settlers and explorers. One of them, Leif Eriksson, son of Erik the Red, crossed the Atlantic Ocean to a place he called Vinland. Remains of a Viking settlement in Newfoundland, Canada, show that Vikings reached North America before other Europeans.

MARCO POLO

Marco Polo was 17 years old when he travelled overland to China from Venice in the 13th century. He served the Chinese Emperor Kublai Khan for 17 years. On his return, he wrote about what he had seen. He told of fabulous riches as well as coal, paper money, gunpowder and printing; things no one had ever seen or heard of in the West.

FINDING THE WAY

* The magnetic needle of a compass points north.

* A sextant helps you calculate where you are by measuring how high the Sun or a star appears to be at a particular time.

TRADERS AND ADVENTURERS

- Captain Cook was a British seaman who explored the Pacific in 1768. He mapped many islands, as well as Australia and New Zealand.

- Francis Drake was an English buccaneer and explorer. He landed in northern California in 1579, and named it New Albion.

- Ferdinand Magellan, like Columbus, set out to find a new route to the East Indies. His 1519 voyage was the first to sail round the world.

- Christopher Columbus wanted to find a new trade route to Asia. In 1492, he sailed west across the Atlantic. Columbus discovered many Caribbean islands.

- Vasco da Gama left Portugal in 1497 and discovered the eastward route to India. He rounded the Cape of Good Hope at Africa's southern tip and crossed the Indian Ocean.

STRANGE BUT TRUE

★ Early explorers believed the Earth was flat. They did not want to sail too far, in case they went over the edge!

THE RACE FOR THE POLES

For a hundred years, explorers tried to reach the North Pole. The American Robert Edwin Peary reached it first in 1909. Huskies pulled his sleds over the ice. There is no land at the North Pole, just the frozen Arctic Ocean.

Racing for the South Pole in 1911, the Norwegian explorer Roald Amundsen beat the Englishman Robert Scott by one month. He also found the Northwest Passage and the magnetic pole.

INVENTIONS

Since the early 20th century, the way we live has changed very fast. Not so long ago, most people lived the same way their grandparents did. A few key inventions, such as the wheel and electricity, have greatly changed the way we live.

THE WHEEL

No one knows who invented the wheel. People living in the Middle East used a horse-drawn war cart about 5,000 years ago. It had solid wheels made of wood. Later, chariots were made with spoked wheels. Now we depend on wheeled transport for nearly everything.

PRINTED BOOKS

The Chinese were printing books more than 1,000 years ago. But modern printing, using moveable letters made of metal, was invented by Johannes Gutenberg in 1447. Books made this way cost less and helped to make knowledge widely available.

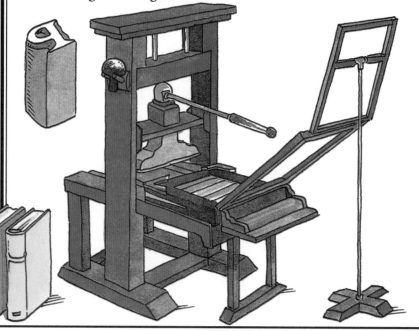

COTTON

American Eli Whitney invented the cotton gin, a machine that separates cotton fibres from the seed, in 1792. The seeds must be removed before the fibres are spun into thread and woven. The separation was once done by hand.

ELECTRICITY

In 1831 Michael Faraday, an English scientist, invented the dynamo, a machine for making electricity. He also invented the transformer and the electric motor.

Electric light makes everything light as day.

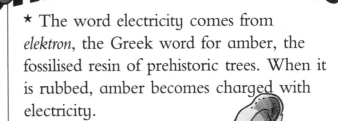

STRANGE BUT TRUE

★ The word electricity comes from *elektron*, the Greek word for amber, the fossilised resin of prehistoric trees. When it is rubbed, amber becomes charged with electricity.

★ American Thomas Alva Edison patented 1,300 inventions. One of his best known inventions was the phonograph, which he thought would be used in offices for dictation.

THE STEAM AGE

James Watt, a Scottish engineer, found a way to make steam engines work efficiently in 1763. His engines were used in factories and mines everywhere and started the Industrial Revolution in Britain. Forty years later another engineer, Richard Trevithick, invented the railway engine when he put a steam engine on wheels.

NEW TECHNOLOGY

Once, the quickest way to send a message was by horse. Then railways were invented and they carried the mail. Now new technologies have changed how people communicate. We send pictures, sound and messages around the world by satellite, and into outer space.

MESSAGES BY WIRE

An American, Samuel Morse, invented a code of dots and dashes for the letters of the alphabet in 1837. The Morse code was used to communicate across long distances by sending electrical signals by wire. Scotsman Alexander Graham Bell invented the telephone. On 5 June 1875, he spoke the first words ever heard on the telephone to his assistant Mr. Watson.

"Come here, Mr Watson, I want to see you."

THE COMING OF RADIO

Gugliemo Marconi transmitted the first radio signal across the Atlantic in 1901. It was the letter 'S', three dots in Morse code. Now three satellites above the Pacific, Atlantic and Indian Oceans relay international telephone calls and transmit radio and television programmes. They also link fax machines and computers together by radio.

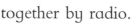

TELEVISION BEGINS

Scotsman John Logie Baird made the first successful television transmission in 1925. The first regular television programmes were made in England in 1936. Now, all over the world, television programmes for entertainment, news and sport are made. Television cameras guard stores against theft and the police use them to control traffic. Scientists use them to explore the bottom of the ocean and distant planets.

LASER LIGHT

A laser makes a narrow, powerful beam of light of one colour. The first one was made by American Theodore H. Maiman in 1960. Today, lasers are used by surgeons and dentists in place of the scalpel and drill. They are used in industry, in communications and in every CD player.

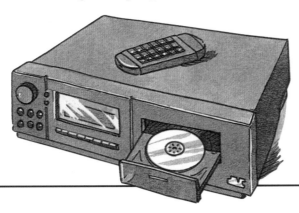

COMPUTERS

The first computers were very big. They filled a whole room. Then the transistor was invented in 1947, two days before Christmas, by Americans Walter Brattain, John Bardeen and William Schockley. Now millions of transistors on a tiny piece of silicon, called a microchip, power today's desktop computers. They make many millions of calculations a second.

STRANGE BUT TRUE

★ The distance between the Earth and the Moon is almost 201,125 kilometres. A laser has been used to measure this to within less than 2 centimetres.

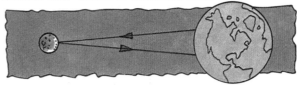

★ The science fiction writer Arthur C. Clarke predicted a system of artificial satellites in 1945, nearly 20 years before NASA launched the first communications satellite, Telstar.

YOUR BODY

A cell is so small, you can only see it through a microscope. This is what some of your cells look like.

Underneath your skin, your body has many different parts. Each part has a different job to do. They all work to keep you alive. Your body needs the right amount of food, rest and exercise to stay healthy and grow strong.

THE PARTS OF YOUR BODY

All living things are made up of cells. The parts of your body are made up of millions of tiny cells of many different kinds. Each kind of cell has a special job to do. Your blood carries to all the cells the food and oxygen that they need to live.

Your brain is the control centre of your body. It sends out orders and receives messages.

Your heart is a muscle that pumps blood out to all parts of your body.

Your lungs bring oxygen to your body. They fill with air as you breathe in and empty as you breathe out.

When you eat a meal, food travels down your throat to your stomach. Special juices in the stomach mix with the food to break it down into a watery mixture. Then the parts of the liquid food your body needs are taken away and distributed by your blood. The waste is pushed out of your body.

BONES

Your body parts are protected and held together by a frame of bones called a skeleton. The main part of your skeleton is the spine (or backbone). The ribs protect your heart and lungs. The skull protects your brain.

Your bones have muscles attached to them. If you want to lift your arm, your brain sends a signal to your arm muscle to pull up the bone in your arm.

STRANGE BUT TRUE

★ Not everyone grows to the same size. To date, the world's tallest man was 2.72 metres and weighed 200 kilograms. The tallest living woman is 2.32 metres and weighs 210 kilograms.

★ Just by taking a single stride, you use over 100 different muscles.

WHY YOUR BODY NEEDS SLEEP

Sleep is a time when your body is resting and making up the energy used during the day. You do most of your growing when you are asleep.

WHY YOUR BODY NEEDS EXERCISE

Everything we do uses muscles. Even when we are resting, many muscles are still at work. Muscles allow your heart to beat, your lungs to take in air and your stomach to digest food. Muscles become weak and flabby if they are not used enough.

SKIN AND HAIR

Skin protects your body against injury and germs. It also helps to keep your body at the same temperature. Hairs grow through the skin on nearly every part of the body, but they are most noticeable on your head.

NERVES

Nerves provide a network of communication throughout your body. When you see something, messages travel along nerves to the brain. Your brain tells you what you have seen. Your senses of hearing, smell, taste and touch work in the same way. Other nerves control muscles so that you can sit, stand and walk.

FOOD

Everyone needs food to stay alive. It gives us the energy to move about and allows our bodies to grow. A healthy person needs the right amount of the right kinds of food. Millions of people do not have enough to eat. More food is produced each year, and many countries share their food with those who do not have any.

WHERE DOES FOOD COME FROM?

Some of our food comes from animals. Farmers raise cattle, sheep, pigs and chickens for their meat. Fishermen go out to sea in boats and catch fish in nets. Fish farmers breed fish in lakes.

Farmers grow crops such as wheat, corn, fruit and vegetables. Some people grow food plants in their own back gardens.

SHOPPING FOR FOOD

Much of our food is prepared in factories. It is canned, bottled, frozen or dried to keep it fresh until we eat it.

In a supermarket you can buy all kinds of food from all around the world.

WHY YOUR BODY NEEDS FOOD

You need food to give you energy. These foods contain sugar and starch. They are called carbohydrates, which give you energy.

These foods contain proteins. Proteins help you grow and keep you fit and strong.

These foods contain fats. Fats keep you warm, but too much fat is not good for you.

STRANGE BUT TRUE

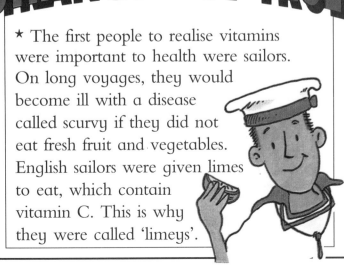

* The first people to realise vitamins were important to health were sailors. On long voyages, they would become ill with a disease called scurvy if they did not eat fresh fruit and vegetables. English sailors were given limes to eat, which contain vitamin C. This is why they were called 'limeys'.

AROUND THE WORLD

Not all crops can be grown in all parts of the world. Some grow best where it is dry and hot. Others prefer plenty of water. People used to eat only the food that grew in their own country. Now food is sold by one country to another.

RICE

Rice is the main food of half of the world's population. It is widely grown in India, Japan and China. Rice plants like plenty of water. They grow best on flooded land, called paddies.

WHEAT

Wheat grows best in dry, mild climates. Most wheat comes from the USA, Northwest Asia, Australia and China. Mills grind the grain into flour for bread, cakes and pasta.

POTATOES

The potato plant came from South America, and is now found in many parts of the world. Potatoes can be eaten baked in their skins or as French fries and potato chips. Sweet potatoes are orange in colour and taste quite sweet.

CLOTHES

Most people in the world wear some sort of clothing. What they wear depends on factors such as climate and culture. Because clothes decorate us as well as protect us, styles of clothing change each year. This is called fashion.

CLOTHES THROUGH THE AGES

Early humans wore the skins of animals they had killed to protect themselves against the weather. Later, people learned how to spin thread and weave cloth.

In ancient Greek and Roman times, from 1000 BC to AD 450, people wore loose, draped tunics.

In the 12th and 13th centuries wealthy people dressed in velvet and fine silks from the East.

In the 18th century, for the rich, clothes became very grand. Men dressed in silk coats, vests and knee breeches. Ladies had hoops under their wide skirts. Both men and women wore huge powdered wigs.

In the early 20th century, people dressed in very formal clothes. Out of doors, men wore frock coats and top hats. Ladies carried parasols.

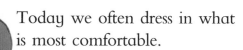

Today we often dress in what is most comfortable.

In the 19th century, a man called Charles Macintosh invented a waterproof coat. The macintosh gave off a terrible smell. Since then, people have found much better ways of making rainwear.

TRADITIONAL COSTUME

Many countries have their own traditional costumes. These are often made from materials that are found locally. Today, traditional clothes are often worn only for special occasions.

The Inuit wear thick, warm, long-sleeved jackets made from caribou skin. Their feet are kept warm in sealskin boots.

Arab people wear long, loose robes to keep off the Sun. The headdress protects their faces from sandstorms in the desert.

The Japanese kimono is made of silk.

Bolivian clothes are made from llama and alpaca wool. A brightly-coloured woollen poncho is worn on top in cold weather.

The Zulu in full battle dress was a fearsome warrior. He wore arm and leg bands made from fur and feathers.

The traditional costume of the New Zealand Maoris is made of fibres from the flax plant.

SPECIAL CLOTHING

The clothes people wear often tell us what they do. You can recognise a doctor or a scuba diver immediately from their uniform or equipment. Some people wear protective clothing for their job or for a sport. Divers wear wetsuits to keep them warm in cold waters.

STRANGE BUT TRUE

★ In 12th century England it was fashionable for men's shoes to have long points. The length of the points showed how important the man was. The law stated that noblemen could wear points 60 centimetres beyond the toe. Ordinary men were allowed only 15 centimetres.

SPORT

OLYMPIC GAMES

The earliest recorded Olympic Games took place in 776 BC. Wrestling was the most popular sport. Victors were given a wreath of olive leaves. The modern Olympic Games began in Athens in 1896. Now athletes from more than 150 countries compete in the summer or winter Olympics every two years.

Each ring of the Olympic logo is a different colour and represents a continent.

FIELD AND TRACK

Gymnasts took part in the ancient Olympic Games. Both gymnastics and athletics are important events in the modern Olympic Games. Races of up to 364 metres are called sprints. Runners use shoes with spikes that grip the surface of the track. The marathon is the longest race. Runners compete over a 40 kilometre course.

WINTER SPORTS

Skating on ice began in Scandinavia, probably in the 2nd century. Ice hockey was first played in Canada in 1885. Not all skating is on ice: roller skates and skateboards can be used almost anywhere. Ski Jumping is a spectacular sport. The skier flies more than 146 metres through the air before landing.

There have been sports competitions since the times of ancient Greece and Rome. Running, jumping and wrestling matches have been organised by most societies since then. Many of the most popular sports were first played in the 19th century.

BAT, BALL AND RACKET

★ American football started with a match between Harvard and McGill Universities in 1874. The annual contest to decide the best professional American football team is called the Super Bowl.

★ The most popular game in the world is football, also called soccer or Association football. Competing countries play against each other every four years for the World Cup.

★ Baseball is played with nine-player teams. The batter tries to hit a thrown ball and run around four bases before the other team can tag him 'out'.

★ In cricket the batter hits a ball that is rolled or bounced along the ground. Then he scores points by running back and forth between two wickets.

★ In tennis, modern rackets have made it a very fast game. Champion players can serve the ball at 208 km/h.

STRANGE BUT TRUE

★ Early versions of football and golf were played in China in the 3rd or 4th centuries BC.

★ The marathon celebrates Pheidippides, the messenger who ran from Marathon to Athens to bring news of the Greek victory over the Persians in 490 BC.

★ The Olmecs in 10th-century Mexico played 'pok-ta-pok', an early version of basketball that used a fixed stone ring and a solid rubber ball.

IN THE WATER

People of any age can learn to swim and dive. Many people sail, canoe or row in their spare time. Big waves give surfers a thrilling ride.

HOMES

Our homes are built from various materials and in many shapes and sizes. In cities, people often live in apartments built of steel and concrete.

In the past, houses were usually built of materials found nearby. Each country has its own style of houses.

THE FIRST HOMES

The earliest people lived in caves. Later, they made huts of mud, grass or reeds. Then they learned how to make houses from blocks of earth or animal skins. As time went by people built stronger houses made of stone.

HOW PEOPLE USED TO LIVE

By Greek and Roman times, houses were quite large. Wealthy Romans built splendid villas with running water and baths. In the Middle Ages, houses were built of wood and had just one or two rooms. Everyone, including the animals, crowded into them to live, sleep and eat. Homes of the rich were more elaborate. They were usually built of stone and had many rooms, each for a different purpose.

HOW WE LIVE NOW

Modern houses and apartments are very comfortable. They have different rooms for people to sleep, eat and relax in. Heating systems and insulating materials keep our homes warm and cosy. Large windows make them light and airy.

In the past, the Inuit used blocks of pressed snow to build igloos.

HOMES THAT MOVE

The Plains Indians of North America lived in skin tents, called teepees. They were easy to take down and could be carried whenever the tribe moved on. The Bedouins of North Africa still move their homes in this way.

FLOATING HOMES

In Hong Kong harbour, thousands of people live on houseboats. They use them as fishing boats in the daytime but they eat and sleep on them as well.

STRANGE BUT TRUE

★ Many homes today have some form of central heating. The Romans used under-floor heating in their villas 2,000 years ago.

AROUND THE WORLD

In North Africa, many houses have thick, mud brick walls and small windows with wooden shutters. The shutters keep out the Sun in the daytime and in the evening are opened so that air can flow through and cool the house.

In the mountains of Switzerland, houses have steeply-pitched roofs so that snow can slide off. The houses are built of wood, which is a good insulator and keeps out the cold.

In Borneo, some houses are built above water on stilts. This makes them safe from snakes and wild animals.

OCCUPATIONS

I n some parts of the world people work to produce their own food and provide shelter for their families. In industrial countries most people work to earn money. Some jobs or occupations are suitable for people who like to work with their hands. Some require many years of study.

PRODUCING FOOD

Many different occupations are involved in producing food. Farmers grow crops and raise cattle for meat. Fishermen catch fish. Millers grind grain into flour, which bakers turn into bread. Other food is processed and packaged by people working in factories. Truck drivers deliver food to the supermarket.

MANUFACTURED GOODS

In industrial countries, many people are employed in factories that manufacture goods. Designers draw up the plans of what is to be made. Machine operators work on raw materials to produce the finished article. Sales people sell the goods. Managers supervise the workers.

PROVIDING A SERVICE

The police, firefighters and ambulance drivers make our lives safer. Transport workers, waiters and hotel staff make life more comfortable and convenient. They all provide a service.

ENTERTAINERS

Some people entertain others as an occupation. Actors, singers, dancers and musicians perform in front of people. Other entertainers make films, write books or paint pictures for people to enjoy.

Teachers show us how to read and write. They also train people to do all kinds of occupations.

HEALTHCARE

When we feel ill, we go to see a doctor. A dentist looks after our teeth. An optician checks our eyes. In the hospital an operation is performed by a surgeon. Patients are cared for by nurses. All these occupations are part of the medical profession.

OFFICE WORK

Office workers usually sit at desks for most of the day. They use computers to keep records, work out problems, and send and receive information.

STRANGE BUT TRUE

★ Mr. Izumi, a Japanese sugar farmer, worked in the fields for a record 98 years. He retired in 1970, aged 105, and lived to be 120, another record.

★ Some people choose really dangerous occupations. A stunt person takes the place of a film actor when a scene involves a dangerous act like jumping off a building.

TRANSPORT

For most of history, riding a galloping horse was the fastest way to travel on land.

Sailboats made great ocean voyages. Then the invention of the steam engine changed land and sea travel forever. Today's transport depends on the gas and the jet engine.

GOING BY SEA

The ancient Egyptians and Chinese had sailboats. Greeks and Romans used boats with oars for war and trade. Explorers voyaging in sailboats discovered and mapped the world. Until the 20th century, vessels sailing the oceans carrie cargo around the world. Then came steamships. Today's supertankers and container ships are powered by oil.

THE RAILWAYS

The French TGV and the Japanese Bullet trains carry passengers at high speed between cities as quickly as an aeroplane. In cities, passengers move around quickly above and under ground in computer controlled trains. The Bay Area Rapid Transit in California was one of the first such systems in the USA. The first trains were steam powered and the passengers sat in open carriages.

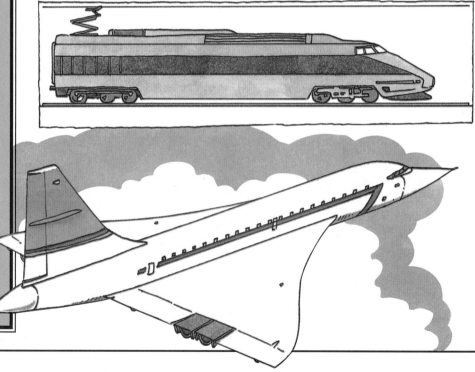

GOING BY ROAD

The first automobiles were powered by steam engines. In Germany, Karl Benz built the first modern automobile in 1885. It had three wheels, a gas engine and a top speed of 14.5 km/h. Today, the automobile is the most popular transport for millions of people.

The Ford Motor Company was first to build 1,000,000 vehicles a year.

The pneumatic (air filled) tyre was invented by Scotsman John Dunlop in 1888, at almost the same time as the first cars. Another Scotsman, John McAdam, invented macadam. This mixture of crushed stones, sand and tar made the first modern roads.

FLYING

Two Americans, Orville and Wilbur Wright, built the first successful aeroplane. The brothers named their biplane *The Flyer*. Its small gas engine turned propellers. In 1903, Orville made the first flight – 36 metres in 12 seconds. Now Boeing 747s, with four jet engines, regularly fly halfway around the world with 400 passengers.

STRANGE BUT TRUE

★ The first air passengers were a sheep, a duck and a hen. Their 1783 flight in a hot-air balloon, built by the French Montgolfier brothers, was witnessed by American inventor Benjamin Franklin.

★ The average speed of traffic today in central London is the same as horse-drawn traffic at the beginning of the 20th century.

SPACE

Once, people thought the Earth was flat and at the centre of the Universe. Now we know it is part of the Solar System. The Earth is one of the nine planets that go around the Sun. Astronomers used telescopes to discover all the other planets.

THE SOLAR SYSTEM

There are four inner planets. Mercury is closest to the Sun, then Venus, Earth and Mars. The outer planets are Jupiter, Saturn, Uranus, Neptune and Pluto, which is farthest from the Sun.

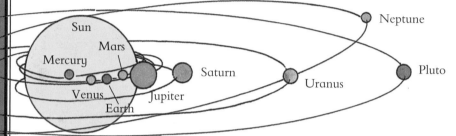

The path, or orbit, that a planet follows is like a slightly flattened circle. This is called an ellipse.

THE UNIVERSE

Our Solar System is part of a galaxy called the Milky Way. Astronomers using powerful telescopes now know that there are many other galaxies in the Universe. Some of the most distant stars have been found because they emit powerful radio signals.

SATELLITES AND PROBES

The first artificial satellite, Sputnik 1, was launched in 1957. Since then, space probes such as Voyager 1 and 2 have flown past the outer planets. Orbiting satellites provide accurate navigation systems for planes and ships and information for weather forecasters.

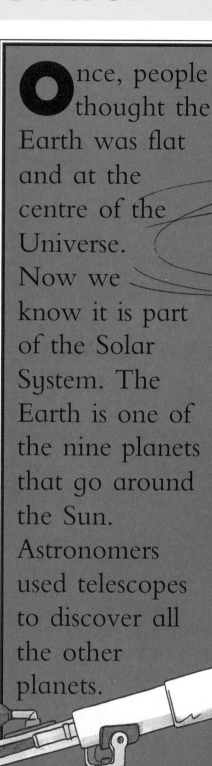

THE MOON AND MARS

In July 1969, American Neil Armstrong became the first person to walk on the Moon. The 11th Apollo mission, powered by a giant Saturn space rocket, took three days to reach the moon. In 1976, two US robot spacecraft called Viking 1 and 2 landed on Mars. They photographed and examined the surface of the planet and looked for signs of life.

Viking 1

THE SPACE SHUTTLE

The Space Shuttle is the first space vehicle that can return to Earth and be used again. Including booster rockets and fuel, it weighs more than 2,000 tons, and can carry 39 tons of cargo, and a crew of seven people. The Space Shuttle is used to put satellites in orbit and for scientific experiments. It has flown a successful mission to repair a damaged satellite.

STRANGE BUT TRUE

★ The moon is about 24,140 kilometres from Earth. It would take you more than nine years to walk there.

★ A star is formed in our galaxy every 18 days. That means there are 20 new stars each year.

SPACE STATIONS

A space station orbits Earth like a satellite. Astronauts and scientists live and walk in it. A space station gets power from solar panels that turn sunlight into electricity. Three crew manned the American space station Skylab before its mission ended in 1974. Two cosmonauts lived on the Russian space station Mir for 366 days.

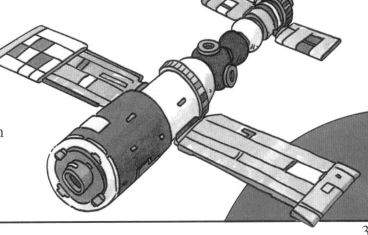

INDEX